To Love the River

To Love the River

Poems by

Siham Karami

Kelsay Books

Cover by Hilma af Klint (1862-1944)
Klint was a Swedish artist and mystic, and a pioneer of abstract art.
"The Dove No. 01" (1915)

ISBN: 978-1-949229-28-8

Kelsay Books
Aldrich Press
www.kelsaybooks.com

For K.,
beloved counterpoint;

And for my children
who are no longer children,
but essential to my survival;

And the many
who helped make this book
and this poetry possible

Acknowledgments

Thanks to these fine publications where the following poems first appeared, some with slight variations:

14 by 14: "The Departure"
Able Muse: "In the Louvre," "Portrait of Her Hands"
Alabama Literary Review: "Unspoken"
Angle Poetry: "My Heart is an Extremity," "Sunset Canyon," "Epithalamion"
Antiphon Poetry: "How Could I"
Atavic Poetry: "Mallwaves"
Autumn Sky Poetry Daily: "Year of the Dragon"
The Comstock Review: "Lawnmowing in America"
Eyedrum periodically: "Last Will and Testament," "On Mt. Sinai"
The Ghazal Page: "Don't Weed Your Wife," "The Superiority of Mud," "The Triumph of Roses"
Hobo Camp Review: "Once upon a Time in Minnesota"
Innisfree Journal: "Labor Day"
Irresistible Sonnets: "The Hawk"
Kin Poetry Journal: "Gently Still Finding You Between"
Lavender Review: "Bird of Paradise"
Measure: "Czechoslovakia"
Mezzo Cammin: "My Lowered Eyes," "Perfume," "The Moment"
Naugatuck River Review: "Edna Hong's Bread"
New Verse News: "Letter to Asma Al-Assad"
Noctua Review: "To Love the River"
Orchards Poetry: "To a Birch Tree," "Common Cup," "Awakening"
Peacock Review: "Out of the Dark, Wild Deep," "The Gift"
The Raintown Review: "Going to Work with a Black Eye"
The Rotary Dial: "Branching"
Shot Glass Journal: "Shopper's Enlightenment"
Snakeskin: "Scarfish"

String Poet: "Nautilus," "Rain Trance," "Touching Down in Paris"
Sukoon Magazine: "The Word for Dawn"
Think Magazine: "Aware," "Mugshot, after the Sting"
Tilt-a-Whirl: "In Egypt," "The Tipping Point"
Unsplendid: "By the Dawn's Early Light," "Good Housekeeping"

Contents

Branching

The Word for Dawn

Fajr: the *j* a mere mirage, light on the tongue,
just melting into *r,* no vowel between,
bluing into nothing but a turning of the lips.
I hear it like a distant motorcycle,
its street lost in a cricket's heartbeat,
and I find it leaking tiny drumbeats from
my son's earbuds fallen from his ear,
buzzing in his sleep. Newborn wasps,
tinny, revving *j's* straight through the *r's*
that rise and thread their little lights
where teeth touch lips and feel the furry *f's*
a darkness, void, a space of hairy night.
A single hair-edge turning from the deep.

Bird of Paradise

The little girl who disappeared
when cut off by her womanhood
now rises like a phantom bird
whose language no one understood

except the birch trees and the wind
and old chairs and familiar stones
long gone, their traces in my mind,
their words now marrow in my bones.

Light in the marrow, iron red,
light on the wings, a diamond glare
against the darkness of the bed,
the arc of flight my only prayer.

And when at last, the shot is fired,
the arrow sails, a shooting star
that lands with what I most desired,
clutched in old hands, bony, poor,

yet fervent. *Young heart of my mind,*
whom I lost and buried twice,
let this scribe now write, though blind,
your history of paradise.

Branching

On tangents piercing vertigo,
multilateral wooden flow—
Sky is endless: simply go!

In spurts and sprints, our conversation
trampolines each light sensation,
connectedness in conflagration.

Let's get out of here, go down
to waters where our words can drown.
Let me verb your luscious noun—

From the elephant shall rise
in the groin between the eyes,
ancient skin and newborn flies.

Terror in the pulse of birth
down the channel, through the earth,
fire bursting from the hearth.

Darker music moves the heart
in rolling waves, its rows apart.
Viewed from space, it forms a chart.

The Milky Way reveals a tree
on which we map its will to be
in reply to "Where are we?"

Trajectories that heave and sway,
gypsy paths and trunks in clay—
illusories of go and stay.

In the Louvre

I spurned the pious upturned face,
the ladies with grey seagull wings
and stern Madonna-visionings,
the man-child's gilded, stilted grace.

My parents needed no reprieve
from mighty Titian's lustborne dancing
women, nude as cows, romancing
well-dressed men. *But let me leave!*

Down to the belly of the whale,
where the Hall of ancient Egypt held
a man's head. I stood rapt, enthralled
by eyes alight with heaven-and-hell

exuding radiant humanness,
a beauty so intense it hurt
like nascent love—a plunge of heart
whose truce with pain shone in his face.

Where have you been?!
                              Oh, I lost track
of time, I said, half-dragged away.
No one sensed my disarray
or how I never quite came back.

Aware

A child's prayers are fragile things
like beetle eyes, mosquito wings,
the weight of something counted on
cast upon the water where
they're intimately close, aware
that all they love could soon be gone,
the pebbles sink, your wishes drown—
and as you watch the ripplings spread,
a spider hanging by a thread
holds a universe mid-air.

Awakening

A.m. waves roll in as distant chatter
and pixelate with dreams along my hull.
Roused by percolating kitchen-clatter,
I float down through the hall, as if more soul
than body, drawn by coffee's pungent incense
and voices murmuring their rise and lull.
I sit across from Daddy's warming presence,
his firefly cigarette, faint foghorn blue—
with radio and Mother's effervescence,
a soft horizon broadcast into view,
our smiles and talk, with toaster-clicks, attuned
to hatching chicks who've nothing else to do
but stir, acclimating to the light
until we surface to the gift of sight.

Lawnmowing in America

Morning aria, oil magic
in a lawnmower craw—
a growing *omm* . . .

Come, iron clang, come,
lowing wail.
I'm a cowgirl gone geomancer
along Magnolia Lane.

An angle, arc, or line
can winnow an acre
on inner glimmer.
No more corn-mangler,
acorn-wrangler.

We wager grace on loam
no crow-caw can ace
nor worm lace,
a warm clime
no ice-claw can maim.

Mow carnal logic.
We win a larger realm:
wine, romance, an elm
awning, a miracle mile-long
lime wing aglow
in new rain.
Crown me, angel—aim low.

The Gift

He came to us where no one knocked the door
and no one entered. We would never touch
because to him, I was still a child
breaking open shyly in the forest,
in my father's cabin, in the river.

I never let my thoughts profess his beauty,
his slender darkness filling me with light
directly through my pupils to the brain
where I closed my eyes. But who can stop
the heart, the drum of life? His very presence

disintegrated me to elements,
directionless, aglow, a fever spreading—
oh my God, don't ever let him know!
One day he gave me this worn little book
and spoke of ancient nations in America

keeping our true bond with lovely earth,
of unseen spirits which I too could feel
like his voice that rivered through me gently.
Alone together—how I dared not think!
How proud I was to never mention this.

The paperback with yellowed pages held
the hour between us even as I smelled it,
old and musty, pressed against my face.
I kept the gift for years, reading it
to find the lost epiphany of human

untouchable, unbearable pure grace,
the Navajo and Hopi taming ghosts,
the flow of river raising up my heart,
a love that tore my hours into shreds:
a constant drowning, always short of words.

To Love the River

You wouldn't like how my delicate arms
flailed uselessly in the rapids,
or the dim green diorama
of death where I spent my oblivion
under the river's ripped shoulders.
You'd love the river, its violence
unimpeachable, its long breath
a single unbroken word
so beautiful it breaks you apart,
ejaculated into eternity, a sound
like your bloodstream echoing through
a giant aorta, the sound
of a galaxy's spiral arms, distant,
yet here! Loud above you, the surface—
and you are no match for this.
You long for the soft march of birch trees
and their attendant wings, dragonflies,
the infinitesimal reach of delicate things.
Like me, you pump extremities
to no avail. The river
may throw us onto a rock
to go on living. We are not heroes.
Our home is a forest of weaker things.
We name this place, wade onto shore,
settle into leaves and conversation.
And in the middle of our little words,
some enormity pulls us deeper
and neither of us can laugh our way
out of this. Nothing else matters.
Its currents shift our pulse, our course.
If I must drown, let it be like this.

Czechoslovakia

The Departure

The railway station's towering old walls
where broken skylights shed half-hearted rays;
a few lone passengers, meandering souls,
discarded photographs a wind conveys;
here a machine drops one dim-reddish apple
while my friend's father gives her meals he brought.
Their laughter echoes off the iron and marble;
I board behind, almost an afterthought.
Her father waves from the fast-shrinking platform,
my father's absence like a missing hand.
Through houses speeding past, I feel its phantom—
its amputated touch trails close behind
and haunts between the eyes, all down the track
as if he knew I'm never coming back.

In Egypt

Our night flight lands in Cairo, Queen of Sand,
whose shutters swallow city lights like quicksand.

Your sister serves us gritty sandwiches
of bread—to meet weight quotas—baked with sand.

We squander hours flagging speeding taxis.
I, the wilting comma. You, the ampersand.

I lose myself in crawlspace at the pyramid—
reduced, like any other grain of sand.

Imagine hoisting these huge stones this high.
Imagine labor measured by this sand.

Ocean-years have worn me down to driftwood,
light and bald. How much more will they sand?

Your relatives no longer want us here.
The weight of family ties, the spreading sand.

Meanwhile treasures beckon to young men.
Just keep digging deeper in the sand.

The ravenous light in Cleopatra's eyes
awaits us all, too—coiled, an urge in sand.

This arrow in my heart is made of glass.
And when I die, who'll sort its pearls from sand?

Touching Down in Paris

Our Egyptair flight lands in Paris rain,
a paradise of grays after the desert
fever-sun burning Cairo's dust
where traces of my heart lie dry and blistered
under stubborn skies immune to clouds.
Longed-for droplets on the window pane
refresh my senses. To land and be uplifted.
Here a mist's fine silk so gently floats
its voile bouffant that I can almost taste
the weightlessness, its carbonated froth
held in thin-blown glass as we alight
inside a silver city where July
is served with crushed ice and a sprig of mint,
the sun a filtered orb sustained within it.

Out of the Dark Wild Deep

We start out famished, shivering, and bare,
clinging to a ragged, dead-eyed bear.

Sans compass, the road becomes our anchorage,
and wind becomes our guide, our law, our bearing.

Another grizzly morning settles in.
Sometimes the gift of life presents a bear.

Can only storms tear me from this stasis?
The heavens growl, lope down in millibars.

You bring flying mystics, Nile-dwelling djinn.
I bring the wilds, and "D. Boone kilt a bar."

These aren't your hunting grounds. But see
this godforsaken cupboard? *Go rob a bear.*

What of library days, my reading years?
The worlds they conjured, lost with Sheikh Zubair.

Archer's fodder, how I need this flight
from grunts and pungent fur. *Skyward, bear.*

Mallwaves

Voices river through the concert hall—
cacophony, a common vowel
dropped like the gravity that binds us all
to earth, to static on the radio
picked up from Jupiter. Somewhere the walls
give way to dynamo, to minds now pooled in stereo,
our words, once lovely, lost in caterwaul.
Strangers' babies, shrill outbursts reflecting
on the passing glass and eyes glazed over.
Our anchors fly away like moths as evening
settles on the lawns, on freeways trafficking
their long hauls through the city. Shadow lovers
disengage from sunset into loitering.
But here the hours are drowned in human sprawl,
in moonless, starless, always-on-the-go
forever day, forever wandering.

Scarfish

I have no moorings in your sea
and yet I live there anyway.
I long to wash ashore, be tossed
on dry and sturdy land long past
the sight of you. Yet here we are
sharing currents and the scar
that brands and bonds us. *Tell me where
we're going.* Makeshift-answers fence
wild horizons, lost expanse,
with words, their simulated shore.
As pain crescendos, still we hold,
no balm but salt and numbing cold.
No buoy rides these endless waves,
but love, its gash, and us its slaves.

Last Will and Testament

For a Street Couple in Pensacola, Florida who died
unexpectedly within days of each other

I swear by this couch-island, our world disappeared
except for each other. Who else would care?

Shipwrecked? We never had a ship.
Wrecked? Two bottles with one message, sealed.

What is the sky? A ceiling they can't take away.
We'll take our roof with us wherever we go.

I only laughed to make you laugh.
How ridiculous the bankers' options are!

We staked out property up on the moon.
Craters, Mare This, Mare That. Tranquility.

In your eyes, I was for real. But you?
My fantasy, my float on New Year's Day.

Then it sank. The earth washed you away.
A morning or a night, they all turned out the same.

Parades of workers, puffing, plugging, beeping.
And bags dripping upside-down.

The moon hid its blurry real estate.
Our moldy couch became a monster, groaning.

Our tarp hung like a joke. And yet your lips,
still parting in my mind like yesterday,

move to form a word, your eyes their voice
and now this blood rushes out to answer—

At the Greyhound Station

We give up hitchhiking and shuffle in,
staring off in opposite directions,
the lotto tumbler turning, turning,
the brown slush lapping at our feet

before the steamed glass door can swing again.
Neither of us can find the missing map
to guide us back to holding hands and smiling.
I draw a blank. Again your eyes withdraw

their fire and water. Again the ticket lost,
the wandering begins, the pencil leads
filling in the random blanks. Again
our conversation hovers in the air,

its breath turns into steam, the steam to slush,
the ugly child of snow. There's no clean break,
only static between stations. Pretend, then, to be stone
unmeltable, pretend to be a man

who never needed anyone, a god
of purest thought, a Plato of the road.
And I will leave, eyes grey as sullied snow.
Neither of us has a place to go.

Labor Day

A foghorn sobs its ghostly passing through
The sun's descending carnival of skies,
While mountains float, untouchable, in blue.

Our yard dips steeply to the street below
Where playing children's distant squealings rise.
A foghorn sobs its ghostly passing-through.

Smoking coals char slabs of barbecue:
The year's last pungent cloud, last crazy flies—
While mountains float, untouchable, in blue.

My stomach clenches for the touch of you
that's almost here. If I could exorcise
The foghorn-sobs, their ghostly passing-through,

Mocking every heartbeat. Is it true
The presence lingers though the bond unties?
Do mountains float, untouchable, in blue?

And what good will it do me if they do?
Inscrutable, insatiable goodbyes
Whose foghorn sobs their ghostly passing-through,
Whose mountains float, untouchable, in blue.

Czechoslovakia

What border on this landscape fools the sky?
A countryside will not refuse the sky.

The heavens spread in glossies on a table—
They told us this is how Prague views the sky.

Find the Little Cloud near giant Pegasus:
Andromeda, in chains, whirlpools the sky.

Were you there in 1968?
The crystal ball, crowds shouting *choose a sky!*

When our train stops, a frozen clump of night
Darkens all the finest jewels of sky.

The conductor says *Your destination's here.*
Bundle your children. Go accuse the sky.

Who can stop the wind from blowing through?
A distant farmhouse. Prayer. The hulls of sky.

Twenty dollars turns the stove and wheels.
Do our petty bribes amuse the sky?

At the station, weeds devouring iron.
An old guard wistfully patrols the sky.

Czechoslovakia, Siham, does not exist.
Don't you read your charts, the news, the sky?

The Hawk

The Year of the Dragon

My parents' fire spent, time seems to drag on
until the cosmos, smoking, spawns the dragon.

All my waters burning. Every look a flare.
Every boy I love turns me to dragon.

Stretch your wingspan's luck between two rivers.
One, an ancient stream. One, a pipe to drag on.

Stalactites stab me, living in this cave—
to leave or enter in, pass through the dragon.

The marrow of all living things is soft.
The marrow of the universe is dragon.

Einstein, stumped. The Theory, elusive.
Beneath their grand equations skulks a dragon.

The daily drip-drip-drip of tedium
feeds the growing fires of the dragon.

I sit alone each night and dream escape.
Then wake each dawn to stroke the seething dragon.

We're at each other's throats. Why stay together?
Old friends walk off and shudder. *It's the dragon.*

You smile and whisper in my ear, *Siham, I promise.*
O garish words! You made me kiss the dragon.

Going to Work with a Black Eye

Don't ask me how I got it. Let's just say
a human storm made landfall, did some damage—
last night's souvenir now on display.
Through makeup, morning blur, its sordid image
blares. I down my coffee, catch the bus
and squeeze myself between the silent crowd,
their eyes in screen-save mode, oblivious.
I know this trance, a temporary shroud
which at the stroke of eight just disappears,
my eye's dark tell-tale tatters thus exposed
to snag right on our humming office gears.
But no! Sweet nothing, normalcy-imposed.
Give me your files, your make-work, your routine.
Anesthetize me, daily grind machine.

My Lowered Eyes

My lowered eyes, my softened tone,
my borders walled for you alone
(no friend or kin would dare intrude),
our twosome built on solitude,
a touch of silk, a love of stone.

But never was I Adam's clone,
a missing rib, an ancient loan
whose full repayment must include
my lowered eyes.

My heart turns to its wild unknown—
no soul can be another's throne.
Of turf and pride you'd strip me nude,
my vision scorned, but not subdued—
as it takes flight, I must disown
my lowered eyes.

Good Housekeeping

See? No ego.
I shine his den, hide his kegs,
sop up his odious gook *(ugh!),*
dig up gunk, snip ends,
pound dough, dip in eggs—
ding dong!— I spin
his souped-up engines,
hug kids, push edges,
spook punks, hook-up hunks,
pose in pink, keep
skin-deep spunk.
I hop on, shop on, drop
goods, dues, shoes.
I spike his pho, dish
his hound dog hog *(oink!).*
He nips gin. I design pseudo Nikes.
He does no good. I do Hong Kong,
keep going, going, done!
Signed, She-King Kong.

The Moment

I'm leaping off a cliff into your eyes
for love, which all the odds say you'll reject —
but higher risk portends a greater prize.

Don't waste a moment with the how's and why's.
Failure is a life one can predict.
So I'm leaping off a cliff into your eyes,

a fledgling bird who either falls or flies,
defenseless from the hurt you could inflict,
a higher risk. And so is what I prize,

a greater love that bares its heart, defies
all warnings, finds a route far more direct.
Don't leap off that cliff! Yet in your eyes,

a sign of light? A spark we recognize —
delicious *we!* — no others could detect.
This greater height— the silence, risk, the prize

unbearable. My being almost dies
when every voice but mine is somber, strict.
Still leaping, now I feel the cliff of eyes
beneath my risky wings outstretched, my prize —

The Hawk

I free myself from my domestic cave
with a basket full of laundry and the wind
and great cloud-shadows passing overhead.
Through flying sheets, the sun appears—a wave
of momentary freedom, and my blood
surges from the roots. But at the line,
I feel a presence suddenly behind
my shoulders, moving closer than he should.
We turn our heads. Our gazes join. The rope
shivers in his talons' grip, a king's
demeanor on his face, fine hackled wings
clasped against his stately form. Then *swoop*—
I watch him soar and perch atop a tree
to scan the world in rebel majesty.

Don't Weed Your Wife

What's this? My shredded heart I'm sewing up.
Our love's old garden? Weeds are growing up.

So where's your new apartment—sixteenth floor?
I've brought wildflower seeds. *Going up?*

You're nervous? A bouquet of dandelions!
(I notice a young woman showing up.)

We should have weeded out the nasty moments.
Now all we have are seed-heads blowing up.

An hour alone together's all I ask.
Embrace a field of larkspur billowing up.

She looks so cultivated. Peach-painted skin
And angel-eyes. Behold her halo glowing up!

Call me henbit, foxtail, witchgrass, thistle.
I'm wild and everywhere. Tiptoeing up . . .

You've done it too—at 3 am, I'm writing,
And you would wail, *What are you doing up?*

It's only fair. Your dainty lily patch
Is strangled by my knotweed, arrowing up.

Shopper's Enlightenment

Through ceiling scaffolds, lines of light fluoresce
their distant buzzing. Sentry black globe-eyes
patrol the ordered pretense of largesse,
a city built of landscaped merchandise
I gather with the swarms. We look for buys,
which piece by piece move from that world to ours.

Outside, a full rebellion in the skies
shapes the darker clouds to giant towers
reflecting embers of the sun's last blaze.
Its blood-orange, yanked by wind-waves' swift riptide,
now gilds our plastic bags with piercing rays.
Mesmerized, I leave my cart to glide
across the lot with my forgotten things,
a dazzled wasp who neither flies nor stings.

Letter to Asma Al-Assad

As you were shopping for designer clothes,
My child was tortured by your husband's thugs,
The price to keep his job to buy you shoes.

Because we stood and chanted, *We refuse*
This tyranny! the bodies piled like jugs
While you were shopping for designer clothes.

He fights with tanks that no one can oppose.
From neighbors' rooftops snipers sink their slugs.
That's the price he pays to buy you shoes

That walk in the machinery of a ruse
To hide the human rubble as he shrugs,
So you can keep on shopping for the clothes

That lighten up his heart before he mows
Down men like grass, lets hospitals pull plugs—
The price to keep his job to buy you shoes

Whose path is getting rougher as it goes
Down darker where you can't tell men from bugs
And guts are dropping on designer clothes
And God knows where you're stepping with those shoes.

Mug Shot, after the Sting

His face unsettles, draws apart the pieces.
Eyes unmatched, they put off, draw you nearer.
One reflects your image in its mirror.
One reserves a need for darker places.

His brows sublime, his sorrows have no peer.
Dead serious as sentry and a fence,
his deeper look won't stand in his defense.
The spotlight snares him. So the buck stops here.

Here when antlers lock, the earth shuts down,
metallic clockworks slam against the heart.
His handsome face contorted by the breach,
the sudden loss of breath and then of ground—
but what he'd give to smell a patch of dirt!
The grace of trees forever out of reach.

On Mt. Sinai

i.m. my father

For the nuances of fire,
he smoked, ignoring what wore down invisibly.
I averted my face from tobacco souring our air, and shrank
before his tower swaying in a gentle quake
as he shared balance charts, accounting notes, ledger columns.
Insurance litanies became last rites for what they couldn't cover,
the sticky valves, pump heaving, until
at a certain point—the *punkt.*

At high noon, he stood on Mt. Sinai
Golf Course with friends. It crossed
over his expanse of smile,
darker than humus under the green,
when he joined the ball's arc
driven into the air,
ascent, descent, a sine wave
of all he was, down through
his solo terminal, where
innocent, he fell
as a man must fall. For God,
a counting. For us,
an outline of the mountain
blue on our horizon.

Common Cup

Nautilus

Awake within a sea of sleep,
buoyed by the rhythmic tides
of breathing out and breathing deep.
The grey-walled waves and dark divides
surround my heart, an ark of ache
whose bruised and buried pulse abides
in shudderings of give and take.
How long these souls, oblivious,
will float in dreaming while I break
beneath the weight of being *us,*
how long my old world, torn away,
will haunt this diving nautilus,
is measured in the heave and sway,
in storms that drown what I would say.

How Could I

What years I lost without you, just for him—
You, who brought me poetry, who laughed
as if the glass I broke was never shattered.
You, whose easy overlooking eye
spurned the petulance of petty things
that cut our soft anemones inside.
Simply mother, grey-brown-headed wren,
whose breezes, hardly felt, became our air,
always unpresumptuously gentle
doing what you did without announcement,
the coffee made, the kitchen bright, the table
set as we presumed it would be set,
a tone of reassuring daily-ness,
a background pulse, a barely noticed love
through peaches, pickled cucumbers, and bread,
a redolence of roast, a lovely brimming
of ordinary dreams and conversation.
You, who turned the soil of your own beauty,
planting aromatics—nothing fussy,
wild with overgrown, green-smelling leaves—
no trellises, just straight out of the dirt—
a shoot of living breath, and worn-out hands,
a presence in the rooms we left behind.
You who without saying, understood.
And still would, could I only have you back.

Unspoken

My father let his silences be words
whose meanings fluttered over trunks of sound.
The pauses held so much more than we heard.
Our path traversed the woodwind forest down
to river-cymbals crashing over rocks—
applause that freed his rising baritone
and filled our shared acoustics in these walks—
his stutter gone, his tongue controlled instead
by his soaring voice—old childhood shocks
now buried deeper in the riverbed.
Our sense of boundlessness brought mind to mind
with reverence for what he left unsaid.
It kept a space—our closeness undefined,
a wind still moving all he left behind.

To a Birch Tree

Remember, my old white-trunked companion,
when I tore off your bark, peeled it down to deerskin
where my family wrote messages we'd wedge
inside the cabin's screen door?

Your leaves sifted light and winds,
a conduit between the earth and sky,
and the outhouse's fecal larder buzzed
with its gang of bowery blueflies hanging out.

In deeper, dragonflies jousted
behind medieval pines' cathedral dark.

Then I turned to take root in a new
earth tempered by human hands,
producing perfumed mangoes, tall cane stalks,
guavas bursting open, stands of palms
like Roman columns—crowned,
and hung with crisp-juicy red and yellow dates.
A garden—sacrilege to call it woods.

Yet unkempt forest still surrounds my heart
where you, guarding sprays of weeds
and grass no scythe could conquer,
harbor wasps and insect dulcimers.

Here in your wild heaven, overgrown,
the sight of white trunks shivers through like love.

Portrait of Her Hands

i.m. my mother

To stop my sermon-squirming on the pew,
you gave me your limp hands, playmates from you
that let my fingers slide inside their V's,
their moonscape backs, distended veins and seas,
and navigate the landmarks recognized
as *Mare Crisium,* and knuckles prized
like sailors' knots, a ragged tapestry,
your cryptic manuscript's calligraphy
I smudged with fingers' fidgety demands,
as all your children's ways inscribed your hands
that I ignored until I found my own
blue veins and kinks hung loose above the bone,
and ridges tracing mother-runes sewn in—
your signature embroidered on my skin.

Common Cup

The angels came down in the form of snow
and wrapped me in their world, away from all
the grownups laughing just behind the door.
Soft flakes glittered in the streetlamp's glow,
and so was night and loneliness made small
enough for my companion-thoughts to soar.
Until I felt your penetrating gaze
jostle me where feelings intersect
with words: *You're just like me. I am like you.*
The years between us silenced in a blaze.
Marooned together by that disconnect,
our sisterhood was galvanized, a coup
transforming how we walked, with footprints deep
in snow, our witness to the bond we keep.

The Superiority of Mud

The sky kissed earth, attracted by her ferrous roots,
Their lightning-love igniting a fanfare of fruits.

So here we are, our breath of God sunk deep in mud—
For all the bluster of our leaves, a pair of roots.

We let our dreams go slack, our days slip through the cracks,
Yet from the compost of our laissez-faire grow roots.

You made me out of fire, but made him out of mud.
A jealous Satan stripped us down to bare roots.

What djinn could hold the calculus, graph sine or tangent,
Or find the power of x or its square root?

We love our bodies' luscious touch of the divine,
A bond that hums in the voltaic hairs of roots.

From mud comes wood and leaf, then pen and ink.
We trace the generations down through shared roots.

The alchemy of things begins inside the forge.
We are the dross, the engineers, the dare of roots.

To heal the pains of physics in our blood and bones,
We harness ginseng, ginger, burdock, arrowroot.

Once Upon a Time in Northwoods, Minnesota

From a half-mile up, you hear the Brule River,
its water-scent rising over fading cabin
resin. And here I stop at the Cathedral
of tall fir columns, an island of stillness clearing
our thoughts from cluttered summer
with the cool incantations of trees.

I join the festival of white birch trees,
a wedding procession down to the river.
Deerflies' twang and wasp harmonicas, a summer
orchestra follows us from the cabin.
Soon the river's clamor scours a clearing
for its incessant rush, a sound cathedral . . .

A statue on a boulder, I must break this cathedral,
its echoing my father's calls, the murmuring trees.
Dive in! Fight upstream! Clearing
my throat, I hurl my whole self blind into the river.
It muscles me into its underworld cabin—
a silent unraveling—then disgorges me onto the shore of summer.

Where's Mother? Everyone?—oblivious as summer,
they never look from their distant cathedral.
Back at the cabin,
I slam the screen door. Only the trees
and dragonflies seem to know the river
brings death as a stock-still clearing.

When night deepens into a clearing,
my father wakes us: *Northern Lights!* Summer
curtains wave across a river
of stars. This is his cathedral,
high above the trees,
luminescence drowning our little cabin.

Years staved me in since I last saw the cabin—
though kerosene pungency brings it back, clearing
its place, a floating summer.
Years break everything but the cathedral
where prayers of insects, families, trees
pass through death as I passed through the river.

Now cabin summers weave through city winters
where they're clearing trees for asphalt tributaries;
my heart a riverbed, a cathedral in the woods.

Sunset Canyon

What if my heart, in its slow twilight, lost
all fear, and let me watch its waning bloom
seduce the hour? The clinking glass, a toast
as fine chromatics gild my mountain tomb.
We'd take our time, this final hour and I,
like lovers drinking in their last slow dance.
Our drumbeat, earth; our canopy, the sky;
All else would fade in pure irrelevance.
My passing colors line the canyon's wall,
rock ochres fired in blazing red. Our kiss
uplifts, a timeless draught as memories fall.
It doesn't even feel like an abyss.
So bury these last pulses, death, for me
beneath the sky's resplendent banyan tree.

Edna Hong's Bread

By the Dawn's Early Light

Bright whale's rise in the eastern sea
draws nigh with an easy drawl,
slightly drab, earth's shade behind.

Wandlight's sway gilds
the edges of it all.
Barely heard warbling birds trill,
whistle, bend the still waters
with their tiny weights

'til the whale-star's bling
blares along the wren-grey line,
a daring *yes* hard against the setting night.
Its treble-shine bids
this day greet the wilds
with an inhale gently drawn.

Rain Trance

I love this constant thrumming on the roof,
wrapping me inside its thick cocoon
of sound, a monastery in the rough.
Percussive chants, these waves refresh the bone,
carry in their very pulse a silence—
not an eye, but a collective calm
whose soft crescendo beckons with its cadence.
Through swells of chattering I hear a psalm.
My sense of place dissolves, the clouding hours
disintegrate, my thoughts—mere whisper-heft—
form solo islands in a sea of choirs.
And who or what am I? And what is left
of this world as I drift away, aloof?
Just a constant thrumming on the roof.

Gently Still Finding You Between

spirals in the shell you left behind,
on staircases, in tiny unseen rooms,
interstices, hidden ventricles,
auricles collapsed and yet alive,

imaginary origami hearts,
a nautilus still pumping through the days
that lost you in their downy underside
like sepals undernoticed, or a potted
cactus near the window no one looks through.

What liquids had been stored in you for years?
Love or some restrained guffaw or blooming
should have burst through sediment and rock.
So much to say, we found no way to talk.

The droplets never touched the cavern floor—
bonded to the minerals that melt
in geologic time, you are no more,
although your shape still shadows my old thoughts:
a gentle tapping on the window's cold.
A film of rain coats footprints on the stairs.

The Triumph of Roses

The young earth hardened, heated, split, then froze,
but still could not disorient the rose.

We kept the emails, pictures, cards in files;
But where, how, could we document a rose?

Sleepless without you, nights etched in glass,
I see the world through temperamental rose.

They grace the small, as if to taunt the great—
such beauty humbles monuments and pharaohs.

The poetry of petals is the science
 of opening the hub, the pent-up rose.

With thorny vines like pythons winding hard,
Who crushed what seemed so permanent . . . the rose?

Immobilized with longing, I sent hope
and dreamed of your reply—but you sent arrows.

One day the oceans will turn flaming orange;
The sky, a dusky firmament of rose.

A man may practice cruelty and thrust
But these will never circumvent the rose.

Your love, Siham, dispersed by wasps and wind,
returns fecund and innocent as a rose.

Perfume

He searches for *Arpège,* wants to bring
the ancient thirties heady from the grave,
atomizer moments, a slender butterfly
proboscis dipped in auras, rainbow
divining rod on my grandma's musty dresser
where the chemist's oils of fern and orchid
exude through tremolo and organ pipes,

and float like hymns, soprano in the loft,
whose resonance is meaningless to him.
And had he known it made me think of mother,
mink, pumps, and off-white cotton gloves,
her lipsticked mouth that smelled of wine
after communion mixing with the lily
petals, lilac dripping through the air,

would he have kept searching through the stores,
discussing with salesladies at great length
Neroli oil, *Lanvin,* and *Vetiver?*
To him, it was Patricia Nixon's choice,
always smiling as she turned to wave
ascending onto Air Force One. With dark
untouchability, a brightness brimmed

to last, bottled in a rich mossed cellar.
To open it would burn us with its dazzle
splashing blue and gold, a newborn sky
which he says happens in America
and maybe Paris. Smell the open doors
freshening his world. And to bring back
the night we soared, each other's fragrant mix

of myrrh and amber thighs and cedar boughs,
his frankincense a shadow in my throat,
a tongue of sweat and pheromone and pearl,
mouths where pulsing jellyfish lay bare.
He would bring back the iodine and salt
and sticky smudges and my tangled hair,
musk and *Je Reviens* clouding the room

in the cheap motel with its tidy
whiff of smut, its dingy coverlets.
Or bring back the sarcophagi of pharaohs
wrapped in muslin soaked in oil of oud
recalling luscious ruts and queens aroused.
Or wives of Presidents naked in their beds,
their satin sheets stained yellow with *Arpège*.

Epithalamion

Bring the forests crammed with leaves
A-shimmering with light—
Shoo the starlings from the eaves
In crazy startled flight!

Jump the guns and rouse the roosters,
Fill the ground with straw.
Marry rockets to their boosters,
Then lay down the law.

This is the wedding of Adam and Eve
In topsy-turvy heaven-and-earth.
The snake in the hollow is someone's pet peeve,
The Buddha of barnyards is flaunting his girth.

A dancing geometer's fiddling with squares,
A round ballerina is splitting her hairs,
The car's in a rectangle trying to start,
The moon's playing Cupid, a beam for a dart,
Its target a triangle shaped like a heart
Putting on la-de-da airs.

When vows are exchanged for a loaf and some fishes,
An Internet highway festooned with good wishes,
A cone-headed lobster, a funnel of love,
A cap of good hope in case push comes to shove,
A scoop of fair weather, a teaspoon of foul,
A chorus of ducks with a soloist owl.

May June be your heartbeat,
September your cool,
December your jester
And April your fool.

May dreams be your cloud-cover,
Poems your sun,
The ocean your lover,
Each other your one,

Nighttime your magic
And daytime your pride.
(*Will this ever come
To an end?* asked the bride.

Emphatically no,
Cried Siham in a huff.
*Not till my dervish says
Heavens, enough!)*

In short, with all good things, I wish you the tough,
Like rocks under rivers or views from a bluff.
I wish you the nonsense to get to the truth,
A cup of sobriety, a splash of Vermouth.

Edna Hong's Bread

The path to the Hongs' cabin always trilled
with paperlight wings, gnat clouds,
seedpods hovering, dragonflies abuzz.

In her doorway, fresh bread sweetness
mingled with the choir
of birches' flickering leaves above
as Edna stood there anchoring
the forest spreading over hills.
I ate her dark bread and knew I was
a child of the same forest.

Softly as the tiny wings
no one noticed,
lines creased upward in her face
to her eyes, still reflecting children
and the cauldron days of war,
rushing refugees close to her hearth
to stop the horror.

Here in the woods where wars are tangled
in remembered underbrush, and birches
turn their pages peacefully,
white underscored by dark fir shadows,
she carried wheat transformed, fields felled
and recreated into one hand-held whole
exuding all she was and is and will be

mixed in the winds, light, and swarms that pass
and the earth who swallows all our faith,
the scent of fresh yeast baked
into their teeming moment of death
by fire. They who were nothing but fodder

now light the fields brought into forest,
a redolence between her hands and sun,

as I return to break her bread, a hymn
of what we make of everything
we were and are. And there
where our beloved woods breaks into us,
a longing we believe to be God's marrow
turns solid in the ground.

The Tipping Point

The tipping point before the fire,
The endless walk along the wire
Where right or left could burst in flame.
The mind builds up its certain frame
While far below, the shouts ring, *Higher!*

My feet must tread by inner gyre.
The truth of balance guides the liar
Till one stray moment seeks to name
The tipping point—

A place between the spark and pyre
Where life and death would co-conspire,
The point where both sides seems the same—
What we disown and what we claim,
What we detest, what we desire—
And then the fall. Above the spire,
The tipping point.

My Heart Is an Extremity

Who crowned the heads of conquerors with leaves?
You slam the door. I'm rolling up my sleeves.

We read each other's eyes and almost drown
like gypsies rendered speechless by the leaves.

Then winter strips us down to skeletons:
static, silence, sparks are all it leaves.

What is this archaeology of love,
brushing fragile shards, preserving leaves?

Waking to a gentle blush, we whisper
truth in half-words, all the heart believes.

We slowly die, let loose from the tree,
then whirl in restless, weightless crowds of leaves.

Your hands dry out like parchment on their bones,
but longing for their firm grip never leaves.

The spine holds words together, names the whole
but we extract their meaning from the leaves.

Don't measure time, Siham, by things that fall,
but by the upward thrust of newborn leaves.

Notes

Edna Hong (1913-2007) was, with her husband Howard Hong, among the foremost translators of Kierkegaard's works, for which they amassed one of the largest collections in the world. But I knew her from our cabin in the Minnesota northwoods, where the Hong family and others also had cabins built for summer vacations. She baked her famous whole wheat bread on a genuine Franklin stove in their cabin, wrote many books, and assisted many refugees from the Nazis during and after World War II.

"By the Dawn's Early Light," "Lawnmowing in America," and "Good Housekeeping" are written in an author-invented form in which the poem is written using only the letters in the title, with no word containing any letter in a frequency greater than that with which it is used in the title (variation of a Lipogram).

"Rain Trance" is the winner of a Laureates' Prize in the Maria W. Faust sonnet competition.

"Edna Hong's Bread" was a semifinalist in the Naugatuck River Narrative Poetry Contest.

"Last Will and Testament" was reprinted in two anthologies: *Poems for a Liminal Age* (Sentinel Press), and *The Best of Eyedrum Periodically.*

"Going to Work with a Black Eye" and "Letter to Asma Al-Assad" were also reprinted in *Poems for a Liminal Age* (Sentinel Press).

"The Year of the Dragon" and "The Word for Dawn" were nominated for Best of the Net, and "To a Birch Tree" was nominated for the Pushcart Prize.

About the Author

Siham Karami lives with her family near a woods that reminds her of the beloved northern Minnesota forest where she spent her childhood summers. In addition to writing, she has found creative fulfillment in music (performance and composition) and a variety of visual arts, but now spends time in a newfound obsession with photography, which has opened up a sense of the unnoticed beauty to be found everywhere by simply looking. Her poetry and critical work can be found in such places as *The Comstock Review, Pleiades, Measure, Able Muse, The Rumpus, Mezzo Cammin, Tupelo Quarterly Review, Literary Mama, Off the Coast,* and *Orchards Poetry* (as featured poet), among other journals and anthologies. Nominated multiple times for both the Pushcart Prize and Best of the Net, she blogs at sihamkarami.wordpress.com.